This book belongs to:

ONE
SMALL
STEP FOR
MAN.
ONE
GIANT
LEAP FOR
MANKIND.

—NEIL ARMSTRONG

To all those future astronauts
out there and all others who
reach for the stars! —S.K.

For Dad, who could tell me a lot
about F-14 Tomcats, among
other things! —I.B.

 HORIZON

 ALIENS AR

FIRST MAN ON THE MOON!

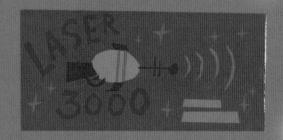
LASER 3000

SPACEMA

SPAC

Text copyright © 2021 by Mach 25 LLC
Jacket art and interior illustrations copyright © 2021 by Izzy Burton

All rights reserved. Published in the United States by Crown Books for Young Readers,
an imprint of Random House Children's Books, a division of Penguin Random House LLC, New York.

Crown and the colophon are registered trademarks of Penguin Random House LLC.

Visit us on the Web! rhcbooks.com

Educators and librarians, for a variety of teaching tools, visit us at RHTeachersLibrarians.com

Library of Congress Cataloging-in-Publication Data.
Names: Kelly, Scott, author. | Easton, Emily, author. | Burton, Izzy, illustrator.
Title: Goodnight, astronaut / astronaut Scott Kelly ; with Emily Easton ; illustrated by Izzy Burton.
Description: First edition. | New York : Crown Books for Young Readers, [2021] | Audience: Ages
3–7. | Audience: Grades K–1. | Summary: "The second picture book from astronaut Scott Kelly follows
his adventure-seeking travels through some of the wild places he's slept!" — Provided by publisher.
Identifiers: LCCN 2020010533 (print) | LCCN 2020010534 (ebook) | ISBN 978-1-5247-6428-9
(hardcover) | ISBN 978-1-5247-6429-6 (library binding) | ISBN 978-1-5247-6430-2 (ebook)
Subjects: LCSH: Astronauts—Juvenile fiction. | Bedtime—Juvenile fiction.
Classification: LCC PZ7.1.K455 Goo 2021 (print) | LCC PZ7.1.K455 (ebook) | DDC [E]—dc23

The text of this book is set in 19-point Cochin LT Pro.
The illustrations in this book were created using Photoshop and a Wacom Cintiq.

MANUFACTURED IN CHINA
10 9 8 7 6 5 4 3 2 1

First Edition

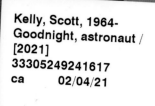

THE SOLAR SYSTEM

SPACE ADVENTURES

ROCK

GOODNIGHT,
ASTRONAUT

by Astronaut
Scott Kelly

with Emily Easton

illustrations by
Izzy Burton

NA

SCIE

TO THE
MOON

Mark

♛
CROWN BOOKS
FOR YOUNG READERS
New York

I was born for adventure,
a blur of motion and energy
times two—

twin trailblazers up for anything.

But even explorers get tired.
We fight sleep like an enemy.

Mom says rest
is our friend.

"If you close your eyes
and dare to dream,
you can go anywhere.
You can do anything.

Goodnight,
my astronauts!"

Beds are boring.
But sleeping high off the ground,
snug in our bags, like cocoons,
takes us a step closer to the moon.

The yard seems awake and alive.
The stars are our shimmering night-lights.

On a family cruise,
our boat rocks us to sleep,
feet to feet
in our matching berths.

When the waves are rough,
we bounce into the air and float
just for a second
like we are in the zero gravity of space.

As brothers grow up,
we chase dreams of our own.
On my first solo adventure
the woods seem so big
and my tent feels so small.
The hard ground cradles me
as the wind lulls me to sleep.

Come morning, I carry my home in a pack on my back, ready to chart my new path.

At school on the ocean,
sailors crowd the ship decks,
learning to steer.
I take the helm,
watching the horizon,
exploring the high seas.

Then I grab some sleep in a narrow bunk
stacked three beds tall.

Sleep tight, crewmates!

Sliding silently through the sea,
we patrol the depths
under the crushing weight of water,
safe in a long metal tube
with no day and no night.
We're secret sentries,
guarding against danger
in our submarine
below the ocean waves,
using the periscope to lift our eyes
above the water.

The skies called me
back up to the surface
to become a floating pilot.
I'm always "go" for launch —
in a jet called a Tomcat,
on a carrier ship.

In a cockpit
on a flight deck,
strapped in tight,
I stand the alert.
But waiting can be tiring.
So a quick combat nap
keeps me ready to fly
whenever and wherever
I'm needed.

Icy woods are chilling,
a frozen world,
like the darkness of space.
We learn to survive
in this dangerous place
and sleep in a snow house,
tucked in between friends.

Our wintry blanket
keeps us warm inside.
But not too toasty,
or our shelter will melt
around us.

Aquanauts learn to be astronauts
living under the sea.

I sleep in a fishbowl,
dreaming of space—
the place I long to be—
as the sea life looks in,
wondering what aliens
have invaded their
watery home.

As I sleep under a clear bubble
in the far north,
the aurora borealis
paints the night sky
with a rainbow of color
from the solar wind bumping into
Earth's outer reaches.
The dancing lights
put on a magical show.

A yurt is the perfect shelter for
a high alpine perch,
Mount Everest Base Camp,
near the highest place on Earth.
There's so little oxygen,
it sometimes hurts to breathe.
More stars than I've ever seen
seem close enough to touch.

After all the training,
hard work, and dreaming,
I finally leave the Earth
on a shuttle called *Discovery*.

An astronaut at last,
I work and sleep with our crew
of seven in a work space
the size of a double-decker minivan.
Spending Christmas among the stars
is an unforgettable gift!

One brother on Earth
and the other above.
One watches over our planet
as the other watches
over our families.
Then we switch places.

Now it's my turn
to live in space for a whole year.
I learn to sleep in a bag,
hanging on a wall as
visions of our beautiful planet
fill my mind and my heart.
Many trips, many missions,
our shared dreams have come true.

Of all the places I've gone
and the places I've slept,
I've come to discover
that home is the best.
In my own cozy bed
with my family nearby,
I sleep soundly,
knowing my mission is done.

So goodnight,
future astronaut!
Start dreaming—
your adventures await.

My dreams have taken me all over the world, from the deepest ocean to the highest mountains—and even into space. Now it's time for your dreams to take flight. Remember: if we dream it, we can do it.

Here are some photos of the places I've slept, on planet and off.

Me at my college graduation in front of the *Empire State V*, the ship we learned to sail during summer voyages.

Mark and me in front of our family home in West Orange, New Jersey—where all our childhood dreaming took place.

Mark and me on our family boat at the Jersey shore.

Courtesy of U.S. Navy

I spent a summer training on the submarine USS *La Jolla* SSN-701.

I flew the F-14 Tomcat off the carrier ship USS *Eisenhower* with my squadron, the Pukin' Dogs.

I trained for space by living and working on the ocean floor, sixty-two feet below the ocean's surface, in the Aquarius Habitat off Key Largo, Florida.

My first mission on the space shuttle *Discovery* was to fix the Hubble Space Telescope.

Sleeping in my quarters on the International Space Station required being zipped into a bag on the wall so I didn't float away while I dreamed.

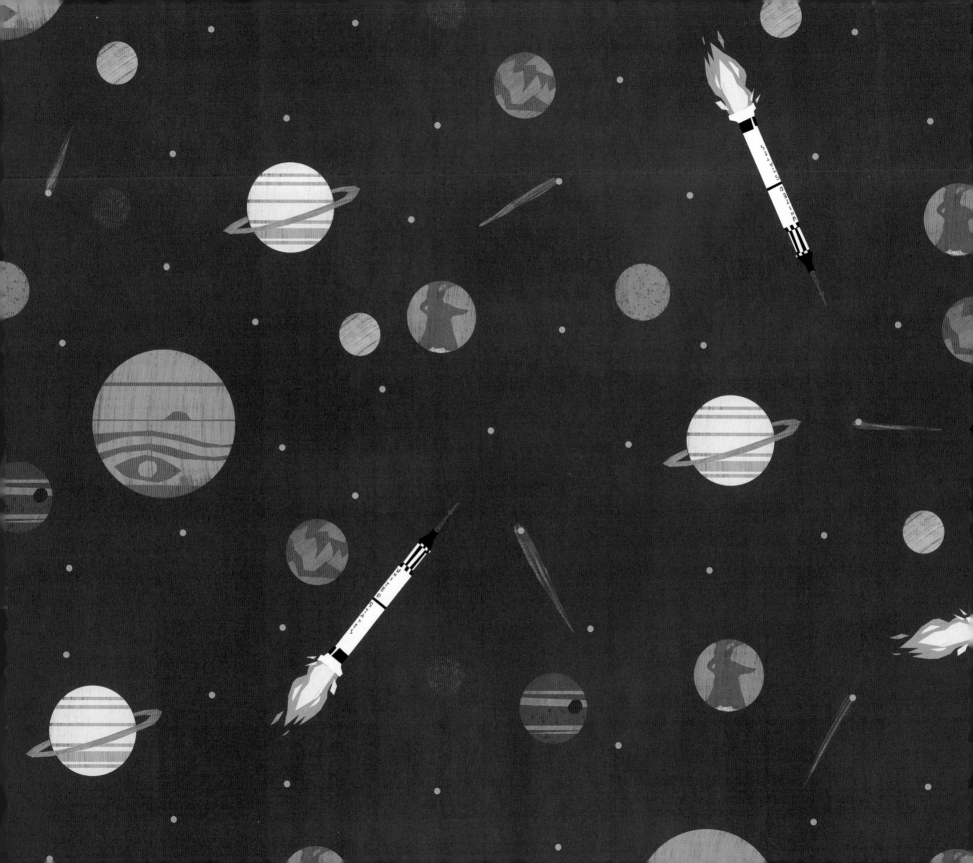